T0142674

When Girls Wear Their Tutus

Tutus

All Their Dreams
Come True

Written by Evelyn Walker

Illustrations by Shane Young

Copyright © 2019 Evelyn Marie Walker.

All rights reserved. No part of this book may be used or reproduced by any means, graphic, electronic, or mechanical, including photocopying, recording, taping or by any information storage retrieval system without the written permission of the author except in the case of brief quotations embodied in critical articles and reviews.

Interior Image Credit: Shane Young

Archway Publishing books may be ordered through booksellers or by contacting:

Archway Publishing
1663 Liberty Drive
Bloomington, IN 47403
www.archwaypublishing.com
1 (888) 242-5904

Because of the dynamic nature of the Internet, any web addresses or links contained in this book may have changed since publication and may no longer be valid. The views expressed in this work are solely those of the author and do not necessarily reflect the views of the publisher, and the publisher hereby disclaims any responsibility for them.

Any people depicted in stock imagery provided by Getty Images are models, and such images are being used for illustrative purposes only.
Certain stock imagery © Getty Images.

ISBN: 978-1-4808-7353-7 (sc)
ISBN: 978-1-4808-7354-4 (e)

Print information available on the last page.

Archway Publishing rev. date: 01/18/2019

When Girls Wear Their Tutus

The girls loved to wear their tutus every day.

Each morning they would wake up! Put on their tutus, it feels as they could achieve anything.

While in a deep sleep one day the three girls, began to have dreams. One was picking flowers, for hours and hours. The other girl was dreaming of counting sheep repeatedly. While the other girl was dreaming of riding a bicycle while eating a popsicle.

Anything the girls desire, they feel it is possible when they are wearing their tutus.

Tutus make the girls dreams come true.

When the girls put on their tutus, they could
eat all the vegetables on their plates.

When the girls are wearing their tutus,
their feet never touch the ground.

The girls twirl and twirl all around.

When the girls were wearing their tutus, one day
they discovered they could dance like ballerinas,

It was like a dream come true.

It was like a dream come true, when the
girls were wearing their tutus.

The girls feel beautiful!

They also used the potty on their own.

When the girls are wearing their tutus, they become Doctors, Lawyers, and Police Officers.

When they are wearing their tutus, they become COOs and Entrepreneurs.

The girls are a success when they are wearing their tutus.

The girls taught others how to make their dreams come true.

When the girls are wearing their tutus,
they can reach for the stars.

In the big blue sky.

When the girls slept with their tutus on, they became
Teachers, Mothers, Wives and Mentors.

When the girls, are wearing their tutus, they can run faster.

When the girls, are wearing their tutus,
they can jump higher than ever.

When the girls wear their tutus to bed, they sleep all night.

When the girls wear their tutus, they are not afraid of the dark.

All their dreams come true.

Dedication
Radiate
Elated
Ambition
Magnificent
Successful

Written By: Evelyn Walker
Illustrated By: Shane Young

Inspired by my Grand-daughters:

Zoey Stevenson
Zaliyah Walker
Amiyah Walker

Special Thanks:

My Sons who made it all possible.
DeWayne J. Walker Jr.
Darion Walker

My Daughters:
Monique Walker
Marissa Morris

My Grandson:
DeWayne Walker III

The UPS Store #2845 & Staff

Acknowledgements:

My Husband: DeWayne Walker Sr.
My Mother: Dollie Fair
My late Father: Arthur Jenkins

Printed in the United States
By Bookmasters